Canyaking
Adventure

T0045234

Rob Waring, *Series Editor*

HEINLE
CENGAGE Learning

Australia • Brazil • Japan • Korea • Mexico • Singapore • Spain • United Kingdom • United States

Words to Know

This story is set on Reunion Island, a small island in the Indian Ocean.

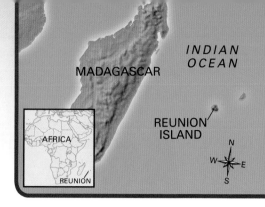

 Equipped for Adventure. Read the adventure equipment descriptions. Then look at the picture and write the letter of the correct item next to each description.

1. _____ A <u>carabiner</u> is a metal ring with a spring closing used with climbing ropes.

2. _____ A <u>harness</u> is a piece of equipment with belts and ties that supports a climber.

3. _____ A <u>helmet</u> is a special hat which protects the head from injury.

4. _____ A <u>kayak</u> is a light, closed narrow boat with space for one or two people.

5. _____ A <u>paddle</u> is a flat tool used to move through water.

6. _____ A <u>piton</u> is a short pointed piece of metal driven into the rock to support a climber.

Canyaking

B **Canyaking!** Read the paragraph. Then match each word or phrase with the correct definition.

Professional kayaker Brad Ludden and his team have a special mission: they want to descend some of the steepest and roughest waterways in the world. They plan to do it while canyaking on the incredibly rugged island of Reunion. Canyaking is a combination of kayaking and canyoneering, and it involves using climbing, rappelling, swimming, and kayaking skills to get through very deep canyons.

1. mission _____
2. descend _____
3. rugged _____
4. canyoneering _____
5. rappel _____
6. canyon _____

a. the sport of exploring deep narrow valleys
b. hilly; referring to land that is difficult to travel over
c. a long, deep opening in the earth's surface
d. a specific and important task or job
e. move downward rapidly
f. lower oneself down a vertical surface using a rope

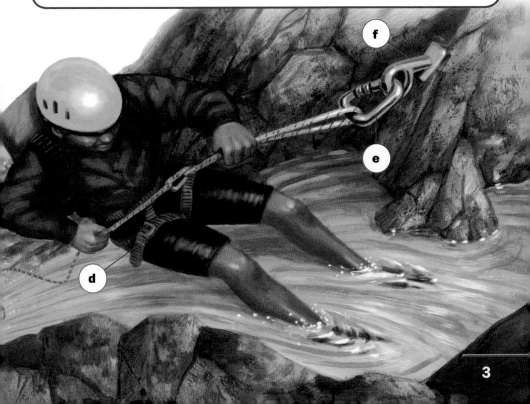

The small **volcanic**[1] island of Reunion in the Indian Ocean might best be described as **paradise**.[2] Its incredible scenery, which features towering mountains, enormous canyons, rugged coastline, and beautiful dramatic sunsets, draws visitors from all over the world. It's the perfect location to try something new and adventurous.

Now, an international team of **whitewater**[3] kayakers and canyoneers has come to the island for a unique challenge. These men are specialists in the sports, but this time they plan to combine their skills to create an entirely new outdoor experience. Whitewater kayakers typically use a kayak to move through fast-flowing water, while canyoneers explore canyons using a variety of techniques that include walking, climbing, jumping, rappelling and swimming. This team has combined these two adventure sports into an incredibly exciting sport called 'canyaking.' This thrilling activity attracts people who enjoy speed, great challenge, and danger.

---

[1] **volcanic:** of or related to a hill or mountain formed by hot, melted rock escaping from the earth
[2] **paradise:** a perfect place that is often considered to be imaginary
[3] **whitewater:** strong, powerful water

 CD 2, Track 05

The team is made up of three professional kayakers: Brad Ludden, Seth Warren, and Ben Selznick, all from the United States. They've traveled a long way for this opportunity and they're definitely ready for the challenge. These three men intend to hike, climb, slip, slide, rappel, swim, and paddle their way across the beautiful green island that is covered in rough **terrain**.[4]

Ludden has plenty of experience in sports as he's a professional kayaker who has paddled in fierce whitewater conditions on several continents. He has been the first person to kayak down more than 100 rivers around the world and has earned two world championship awards for kayaking. If anyone knows what skills one must possess to be a successful canyaker, it's Ludden. He explains in his own words: "Canyaking is a **hybrid**[5] that is using your skills as a canyoneer— in other words, your ability to get through a canyon on ropes and harnesses and sliding—as well as your ability and skills as a kayaker, and combining the two."

---

[4]**terrain:** the natural features of land; the landscape
[5]**hybrid:** mixture

Seth Warren and Ben Selznick also have an enormous amount of kayaking and canyoneering experience. Together, the team of professionals plans to canyak Trou Blanc, which is the largest, deepest, most dangerous canyon on the island. It will be the first time that canyaking has been done on Reunion Island and the first time it's been done through Trou Blanc. Inevitably their adventure will require some careful preparation and intense training—and some expert guidance. Therefore, two other men join the team: the experienced canyoneering guide Chris Schnoller from Austria and a local canyon guide, Christophe Chaume.

Chaume understands the attraction of the island because he lives here. He pauses for a moment to describe the wonderful natural area that he calls home: "Reunion Island, it's a paradise in the world. You have the sea. You have the mountains. You can do a lot of things." The island may indeed be a paradise, but it's one that is full of challenges and dangers for anyone who is planning to cross it while doing adventure sports. The team must be ready for anything.

Saint Denis River

Galets River

Saint Gilles River

Cirque de Mafatte

Cirque de Salazie

Hell Bou

Piton des Neiges

Cilaos

Cirque de Cilaos

Plaine River

Cilaos River

There are three large cirques [sɜrk] on Reunion Island.

The first day of their adventure starts very early for the team. They begin with an early breakfast and then take some time to plan their travels for the day. Chris Schnoller shows them the maps of where they are going and explains the geography of the area in order to prepare them for the drive to Cirque de Cilaos. Located in the center of the island, Cirque de Cilaos is a huge depression in the earth that was formed by the sinking of the land following a volcanic event. The Cirque is one of the three natural **amphitheaters**[6] formed in the rock of Reunion Island. The village of Cilaos, situated about 1,000 meters* above sea level, is an attractive, relaxed village surrounded by high mountains. Chris Schnoller describes what the team can expect there, "It's actually supposed to be the best canyon[eer]ing **resort**[7] in the world." Understandably, the group is very eager to get started on their trip.

---

[6]**amphitheater:** an area with a central point and places for seating rising above it
[7]**resort:** a place for rest and relaxation
*See page 48 for a metric conversion chart.

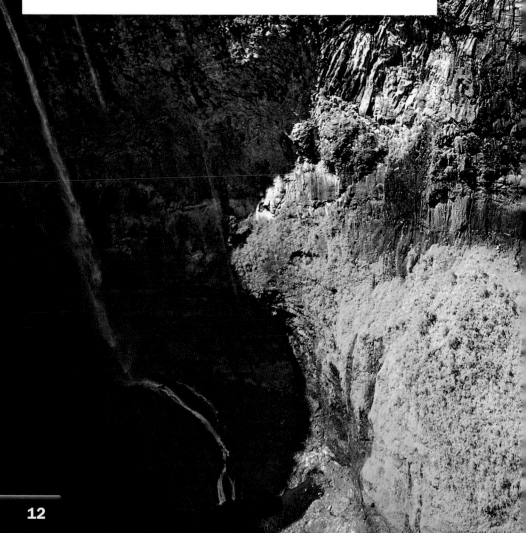

Accessing the best canyoneering resort in the world is also a challenge. The resort is approached by an incredibly high mountain road, which winds up from the coastal plain. With more than 200 very tight bends, known as 'hairpin turns,' it's a thrilling drive through astonishing scenery. The team's first real challenge, however, will come high in Cirque de Cilaos. There, the men will start their canyaking adventure at a canyon known as Fleur Jaune. It's the perfect training ground for their ultimate objective: the Trou Blanc canyon.

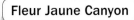

Fleur Jaune Canyon

Once they arrive at Cirque de Cilaos, the team prepares their equipment for the exciting activity ahead. They put on their **wetsuits**,[8] and then attach their ropes and harnesses. They also put on the helmets, which are essential when going down a canyon at top speed. Following these preparations, the men then check their equipment. Meters and meters of strong climbing rope are going to be needed to make the run, and the canyakers need to be certain that every centimeter of it is strong and safe. Therefore, one of the team members spends several minutes checking and winding each rope carefully.

After the men finalize their equipment preparation, Chris Schnoller checks and rechecks it all. In this type of sport, one really needs to depend on the other members of the team, and trust for one's teammates—particularly the leader—is crucial. On this trip, the group of men will put their lives in the hands of Schnoller, trusting his years of canyoneering experience. Seth Warren explains why they're working with Chris. "The guy has been all over the place. I trust him with my life," he reports. "He knows exactly what he's doing [and] when he's doing it. I'm **psyched**."[9] Schnoller is obviously a leader who inspires confidence, and that's of critical importance in this kind of activity.

----

[8]**wetsuit:** a piece of clothing made of rubber that fits the whole body closely; usually worn by people who are diving or swimming underwater
[9]**psyched:** *(slang)* enthusiastic; really excited about something

Everyone is very excited to be participating in this first-ever canyaking trip through Reunion Island's toughest terrain. The descent down the Fleur Jaune is full of risk and challenge, but the team is aware that a successful descent here will help them adjust to each other's skills and bring them one step closer to their goal of canyaking through Trou Blanc.

The Fleur Jaune canyon consists of seven steep drops for rappelling, ranging from a relatively short 15 meters to a breathtaking 45-meter drop. Some of these drops are also covered with streaming water, which means that the men will be going down incredibly steep **slopes**[10] on ropes through very fast-flowing water. At the end of each rappel there is usually a small body of water where the men can land and then swim or kayak to the side of the canyon.

At the first drop, Schnoller starts by attaching a rope to a piton and throwing it over the side of the cliff. Then, each member of the team rappels down the side of the steep slope. Rappelling is an activity that requires great strength and skill. The drops are almost vertical and the water is unbelievably fast—one mistake and a team member could get injured or even be killed. Luckily, they all make it through the first drop safely and without any problems. Now only six more drops to go!

---

[10]**slope:** a surface at an angle, especially of a hill or roof

The team continues working their way through the series of **multiple**[11] drops, lightly stepping and dancing their way down the almost vertical canyon walls. On the steeper drops, they use a rope to rappel down the slopes. On other less steep drops, the men actually use their kayaks and boat down the side of the canyon!

Finally, the team comes to the largest drop of them all—a vertical waterfall that is almost 50 meters high. It's the classic character of waterfalls like this one which draws canyoneers from around the world to Reunion. The waterfall is so high that it seems to go on forever— and it's definitely the greatest challenge of the day for the team.

Schnoller explains the technique they plan to use to descend the waterfall. Using a special type of tie called a 'clove hitch,' he attaches a long rope onto a carabiner which is hooked to a piton inserted into the rock of the canyon wall. To this rope, which extends to the bottom of the waterfall, each member will attach a shorter rope using their own carabiner so they can slide safely down. By using this method, Chris says that everyone will be fine ... but will they? Looking down at the enormous drop down the waterfall, the men must wonder if they'll make it safely to the pool at the bottom.

---

[11]**multiple:** many; plentiful

Predict

Review the information you have read to this point and answer the questions 'True' or 'False.' Then, check your answers on page 21.

1. The entire team will make it down the largest drop of Fleur Jaune. _____

2. One of the team members will be injured. _____

3. The team will terminate their plans to attempt Trou Blanc. _____

4. The team will have a disagreement due to mistrust. _____

Everyone is aware that a number of things could go wrong at the waterfall, and it's the time when coordination among the team members really matters most. Here, at this moment, the team must unite. A mistake at this demanding vertical drop would lead to disaster—not just for one man, but perhaps for all of them.

The first man is lowered over the side of the 49-meter drop. He slips, but then recovers his footing. Slowly, he begins to lower himself down the waterfall using only his upper body strength while he hangs from the rope above. Once he gets used to the experience, he begins to speed up and is soon dropping towards the water below at a relatively quick pace. Then finally, as the rock comes further out from the mountain, he extends his legs back slightly so he can rest his feet on the stone. He then begins sliding down the rock face as if skiing, before finally dropping into a free fall without holding on to the rope for the last few meters of the rappel. He drops safely into the deep water at the base of the waterfall and quickly swims to the side of the waterhole.

One by one, the rest of the men lower themselves down the rope, carefully and slowly, before finally dropping with a loud **splash**[12] into the water at the bottom of the waterfall. It takes time to get everyone down the waterfall, and the atmosphere is intense, but in the end the descent is a complete success. The team now knows that it's ready for the next step: Trou Blanc!

---

[12]**splash:** the sound of something or someone falling into water

The next morning after breakfast, the team must leave Cilaos and walk towards the Trou Blanc canyon, which is over the mountain's edge to the northeast. They look at their maps and plan their route to the canyon, which is reported to be the best place for a canyaking run. Everyone agrees that the best way to get there, although it's a long and demanding trip, is to hike over the highest point on the island, the **peak**[13] known as **Piton des Neiges**.[14]

They begin the long hike over Piton des Neiges, walking up slowly with their heavy packs. It takes the team hours and they must climb several sets of natural stairs that have been made from wood and soil in the side of the mountain. After hours of hiking up the forested paths, the group suddenly realizes that they are already above the clouds, and they've not even reached the top of the mountain. Then finally, they reach the top. From their viewing point at the top of the peak, the team can see far into the distance. Around them, the tops of other mountains appear through the clouds that cover the rest of the island. It's a beautiful sight, but one that falls on tired eyes. The team will make camp here and rest for the night before they continue their trip to Trou Blanc.

———————————————————

[13] **peak:** the top of a mountain
[14] **Piton des Neiges:** [pitɔn deɪ nɛʒ]

It's four o'clock in the morning when the men wake up on the highest point of the island after a well-deserved rest. The sunrise from the top of the mountain is incredibly beautiful and the view is still amazing, but the team can't take too much time to enjoy it. Their plans for the day are going to be even more demanding and more dangerous than their long hike yesterday.

Later, Ben Selznik explains their schedule for the next few hours. "Now that we're here on the top of the peak at six-thirty in the morning," he says, "we are going to go down, we're going to drink a little coffee, have a little bit of breakfast, and then hike another four hours on to Hellbourg while two of the other people from our team go down, get the cars, and meet us over there."

The lovely mountain village of Hellbourg lies in the inner region of the Cirque de Salazie in the northeastern part of the island. Local guide Christophe Chaume has come with the team to consult and bring firsthand knowledge of the canyons and terrain, but he also knows what an important part the weather can play in their plans. Luckily, the forecast is excellent. "It will be a very, very good day with a lot of sun," Chaume says, as he drives to meet the team in Hellbourg. "The perfect day to ... kayak in Trou Blanc. Yes!"

Once everyone reaches Hellbourg, the men get all of their equipment ready for the 40-meter rappel into the huge canyon. They make sure that the carabiners are secure, and that all the ropes and kayaks are in good condition. This time they'll be taking the kayaks down on the ropes too. This is when the canyaking adventure truly begins!

Managing a 40-meter drop while rappelling is definitely a challenge, but imagine doing it with a kayak! The men must bring all of their equipment with them for the trip, which includes backpacks, paddles, and kayaks. When they finally reach the bottom of the canyon, the men get into their kayaks and start paddling through the deep, narrow passage.

While getting around these canyons is certainly a challenge, there seems to be a number of reasons why these men love this sport so much. Selznik explains why he enjoys kayaking in this way: "It's so much more fun going kayaking with a harness and you **abseil**[15] in, and it just mixes things up and gives kayaking a whole new perspective." As the team effortlessly floats through the calm waters that flow through the bottom of the canyon at the beginning of the journey, it's easy to see the attraction to the sport, but one must remember that things aren't always this easy. Paddling on flat water is just basic kayaking; these men are looking to canyak.

---

[15]**abseil:** British English word for 'rappel'

Infer Meaning

Find the word 'perspective' on page 28 and answer the questions.

1. What part of speech is the word 'perspective' (e.g., noun, verb, etc.)?

2. What are the three parts of the word: prefix, root word, and suffix?

3. Look at the words around 'perspective' and guess what it means.

4. Can you replace the word with your guess? If not, guess again.

Professional Kayaker Brad Ludden

Later in their trip through the canyon, Brad Ludden points out that they've finally reached a good spot to canyak and ride their boats down the water-covered sides of the canyon walls. "So we've just made it through the flat section," he reports. "We walked our boats through it, and got to our first slide and it looks pretty good to canyak. It does look though like you could **piton**[16] pretty hard at the bottom of it."

The men inspect the waterfall extremely carefully, weighing the risks and dangers. Between them, they have an enormous amount of experience, and they know what could happen to them if something goes wrong. Now they have one question in their minds: will they be able to descend the waterfall safely in their kayaks? There's no guarantee in this kind of descent at all. Once committed to the fall, they'll have no control over the direction in which they'll go. They'll go wherever the water wants to take them. Crashing into a rock could mean a broken arm or worse. The rough and rugged terrain only compounds the problem; if anything were to happen, emergency **evacuation**[17] would be almost impossible.

---

[16] **piton:** *(unusual use)* Here, the speaker likely means 'lose one's balance' or 'hit oneself upon rocks'.

[17] **evacuation:** the taking of people away from a place, usually because of danger

When going down this first canyaking drop, it's obviously important for the team to be very cautious. They need to minimize the risks as much as possible and make sure that the team's safety is everyone's first priority. Seth Warren is hopeful about their chances, mainly because the **gap**[18] through which the water is flowing is so tight that it's only possible to go down one way. The men will be riding their kayaks down a waterfall that is about a meter wide and traveling at high speeds through a gap that is about one and a half meters wide. In Warren's opinion, there aren't many directions other than forward that the canyakers can go. "There is not much room for diversity in [direction] line," he says. "So hopefully we all make it down it all right." To this he adds with a confident smile, "I think it'll be good."

---

[18]**gap:** space between two things

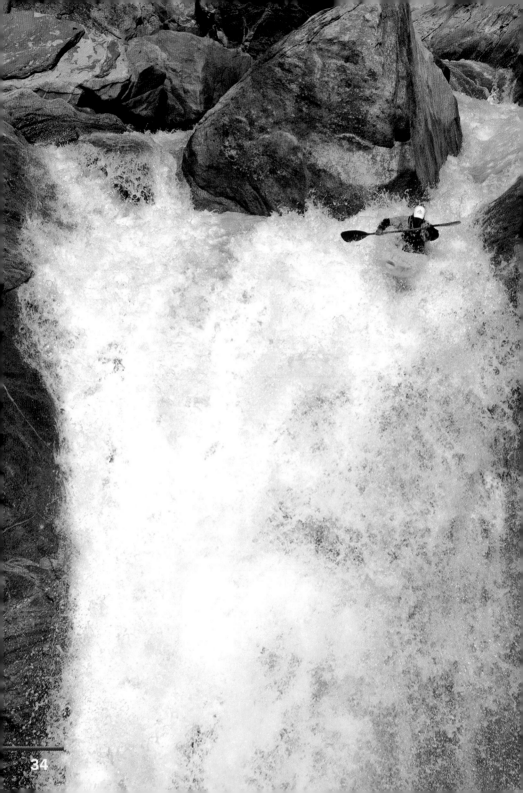

Once the men have taken a very good look at the fall, and studied the technical aspects of getting down it, the first brave adventurer goes down with his kayak. He basically rides on the water flow for a second and then drops straight down into the splashing water below. Finally, his kayak comes back up from under the water and, once he reaches safety, he shouts with delight. The drop is a great success; all the preparation has definitely paid off!

From that point, each man goes down the waterfall at top speed, traveling quickly down the tight gap between two huge pieces of rock. Later, the men continue their canyak through Trou Blanc and it proves to be all they expected. They have a wonderful time hiking, kayaking, and descending through the canyon. This is the reason they came here, for the thrill of canyaking Trou Blanc and they want to be sure to enjoy it to the fullest.

As they travel through the canyon enjoying themselves, one must wonder what the trick is to performing such feats. Ben Selznik explains that he thinks the team's success is due to the fact that they were able to coordinate well. "Sometimes in these canyons, we have multiple abseils [through] tight little **cracks**,"[19] he says. "It's all about group unity, and when that runs smoothly the canyon is **nothing but butter**."[20]

These men certainly make the sport of canyaking look effortless and easy. They go down most of the small waterways of this region of the island by kayak, but sometimes they just slide down the walls in their wetsuits or even jump from the high cliffs into the water. In fact, one of the men even dares to go down a waterfall backwards—in his kayak!

---

[19]**crack:** a line of separation in a material; a split
[20]**nothing but butter:** (unusual expression) smooth and easy

As they approach the final waterfall, the team realizes that their trip through Trou Blanc is complete; they have achieved their goal of challenging Trou Blanc, and they've won. This team of canyakers has successfully combined the skills of canyoneering and kayaking, introducing a completely new sport to Reunion Island. Local resident Christophe Chaume is surprised by what the team has achieved while canyaking. He explains that he really didn't think that it was possible to kayak down such remote waterfalls; he'd never done it before, however he thoroughly enjoyed the experience.

Seth Warren is also satisfied with the expedition's activities and feels that the mission has definitely been accomplished. "Well, we finally finished the Trou Blanc," he says, still tired from canyaking and carrying his kayak. "It was kind of a **bump and scrape**[21] there at the end. We had a great couple of days and a great run, a good group, some good slides, [good] waterfalls." With this he concludes happily, "[It was a] successful mission."

_____

[21]**bump and scrape:** *(unusual expression)* a rough or dangerous experience NOTE: 'Bump' means to hit something with force; 'scrape' means to rub against something rough and receive a mark or injury.

This small group of adventurers has even managed to impress the local residents of the island. Brad Ludden smiles when he explains that most local people didn't think that what the team did was actually possible. "I think the coolest part about it for a lot of us," he says, "was that the day before when we were looking at it, all the locals said it was impossible. And since we've had a lot of people tell us it's impossible, it's kind of fun to tell them that we already did it." Obviously, when a person knows that they've done something that most people think is 'impossible,' it can really make one appreciate it.

Finally, the canyakers put their kayaks on their backs and walk out of Trou Blanc. They've done what they came here to do, and they're ready to leave the island. Some people come to Reunion for its beauty, others come to challenge themselves and test their abilities. These five young men have tested themselves in the most daring of circumstances, and have come out of the experience as winners. They came on their canyak adventure to take on the wild dangers of Trou Blanc, and they did it—with style!

Summarize

Imagine that you are a member of the team. Tell or write a summary of your visit to Reunion Island. Include the following information:

1. What were the team members like?

2. Where did you practice for Trou Blanc?

3. How did you get to Trou Blanc?

4. What did you do when you got there and how did you feel about the experience?

After You Read

1. Reunion Island is described as 'paradise' for all of the following reasons EXCEPT:
   A. large canyons
   B. towering mountains
   C. smooth, sandy beaches
   D. gorgeous sunsets

2. On page 8, what does the guide mean when he says, "You can do a lot of things"?
   A. Canyoneers can choose from many possible routes.
   B. Visitors can enjoy a number of activities.
   C. Adventurers must be careful of dangers on the island.
   D. The island offers too many options.

3. The word 'accessing' on page 12 can be replaced by:
   A. recovering from
   B. enhancing
   C. monitoring
   D. getting to

4. What's the main purpose of paragraph 1 on page 15?
   A. to show how much equipment each member needs
   B. to instruct on how to go canyaking
   C. to explain what the sport of canyaking is
   D. to give an example of how skilled each member is

5. Why did the canyakers go down Fleur Jaune?
   A. to prove their ropes were strong enough
   B. to investigate how dangerous the run was
   C. to get ready for Trou Blanc
   D. to check the temperature of the water

6. What does the writer probably think about canyaking down the 49-meter waterfall?
   A. With a clove hitch, the team should be safe.
   B. The team is taking a big risk.
   C. It will be easy for the experts.
   D. Chris will have to persuade the team to do it.

7. The team travels to the largest canyon on the island _____.
   A. by driving there
   B. by rappelling there
   C. by kayaking there
   D. on foot

8. On page 22, the verb 'falls on' can be replaced by:
   A. is seen by
   B. views
   C. underlies
   D. contradicts

9. Why does the canyaking only truly begin at Trou Blanc?
   A. because it's the best canyon on the island
   B. because it's a sunny day
   C. because the team uses their kayaks
   D. because they start with a 40-meter rappel

10. In paragraph 2 on page 31, 'them' refers to:
   A. risks and dangers
   B. the canyaking team
   C. the waterfalls
   D. the team's kayaks

11. Which of these statements best expresses what Seth Warren says about the drop on page 32?
   A. They will have a lot a space to make up for errors.
   B. The drop will be easier because there's only one way.
   C. They should pass this drop and go to the next one.
   D. Somebody may get hurt on this drop.

12. What does the writer explain about the Reunion Island locals?
   A. They will now use canyaking to get around the island.
   B. They don't want foreigners to go into the canyons.
   C. They doubted the canyakers could reach their goal.
   D. They hope that this new sport brings tourists.

Climb Every Canyon

I t's called 'kloofing' in Australia, 'ghyll scrambling' in Wales, and 'river tracing' in parts of Asia. Europeans refer to it as 'canyoning' and Americans use the term 'canyoneering.' Whatever it's called, it's one of the fastest-growing extreme sports in the world. Canyoneering combines hiking, swimming, and waterfall climbing. Participants begin at the head of a canyon and follow it wherever it goes, which leads to a number of unpredictable adventures along the way. If you like excitement and you're feeling strong and fit, let canyoneering take you to another sporting dimension!

ZION NATIONAL PARK IN SPRINGDALE, UTAH

At almost 370 square kilometers, Zion is the largest and most popular canyoneering site in the United States, and it contains some of the most beautiful mountain and canyon scenery in the world. Zion offers a wide variety of climbing opportunities for everyone from the five-year-old beginner to the

Mount Spry, Zion National Park, Utah

Canyoneering Sites

Location	Where to Stay	Best Time to Visit	Other Attractions	Nearest Airport
Zion National Park, USA	• 30 nearby motels • 2 campsites	June - October	bicycling tours through park	McCarran Airport (254 km)
Copper Canyon, Mexico	• local homes • small hotels	Spring, Fall	local arts and crafts	Los Muchis Airport (322 km)
The Blue Mountains, Australia	• nearby hotels on Pacific Ocean	September - May	snow and ice climbing in winter	Sydney Airport (121 km)

conditioned expert. For the adventurous, the extremely narrow, deep canyons and tall rock towers offer extraordinary climbing challenges. About 2.5 million people visit the park annually and leave with memories that will last a lifetime.

COPPER CANYON IN CHIHUAHUA, MEXICO

This well-known canyoneering destination is located about 560 kilometers south of El Paso, Texas, and contains North America's largest canyon system. A canyoneering vacation in this area is attractive not just because of the outstanding climbing and hiking possibilities, but also because of the people who live there. This part of Chihuahua has many small, isolated villages which appear almost exactly as they did hundreds of years ago. The best way to explore the area is on the back of a horse or donkey. Local families also welcome guests into their homes for a small fee, which adds a very special chapter to your travel experience. A canyoneering trip to this area is a formula for fun!

THE BLUE MOUNTAINS IN AUSTRALIA

Located only an hour from Sydney, the Blue Mountains area, which contains over 400 canyons, offers one of the most accessible and fascinating canyoneering experiences in the world. A popular one-day tour of Australia's own Grand Canyon begins with a rain forest walk followed by a steep climb down to the canyon floor. Then there's a two-hour hike through magnificent scenery and a 20-meter swim to the end of the canyon. The tour finishes with a 45-minute walk up to Evans Lookout which offers amazing views over the Grose Valley. Few places in the world offer such beauty and variety of scenery in such a brief tour.

CD 2, Track 06

Word Count: 417
Time: _____

Vocabulary List

abseil (28, 36)

amphitheater (11)

bump and scrape (39)

canyon (3, 4, 7, 8, 12, 13, 16, 18, 22, 26, 28, 31, 35, 36)

canyoneering (3, 4, 7, 8, 11, 12, 15, 18, 39)

carabiner (2, 18, 26)

crack (36)

descend (3, 18, 31, 35)

evacuation (31)

gap (32, 35)

harness (2, 7, 15, 28)

helmet (2, 15)

hybrid (7)

kayak (2, 3, 4, 7, 8, 16, 18, 26, 28, 30, 31, 32, 35, 36, 39, 42)

mission (3, 39)

multiple (18, 36)

nothing but butter (36)

paddle (2, 7, 28)

paradise (4, 8)

peak (22, 25)

piton (2, 16, 18, 31)

psyched (15)

rappel (3, 4, 7, 16, 18, 21, 26, 28)

resort (11, 12)

rugged (3, 4, 31)

slope (16, 18)

splash (21, 35)

terrain (7, 16, 26, 31)

volcanic (4, 11)

wetsuit (15, 36)

whitewater (4, 7)

Metric Conversion Chart

Area

1 hectare = 2.471 acres

Length

1 centimeter = .394 inches

1 meter = 1.094 yards

1 kilometer = .621 miles

Temperature

0° Celsius = 32° Fahrenheit

Volume

1 liter = 1.057 quarts

Weight

1 gram = .035 ounces

1 kilogram = 2.2 pounds